A Note to Parents

Eyewitness Readers is a compelling new home reading programme for children. *Eyewitness* has become the most trusted name in illustrated books and this new series combines the highly visual *Eyewitness* approach with engaging, easy-to-read stories. Each *Eyewitness Reader* is guaranteed to capture a child's interest while developing his or her reading skills, general knowledge and love of reading.

The books are written by leading children's authors and are designed in conjunction with literacy experts, including Cliff Moon M.Ed., Honorary Fellow of the University of Reading. Cliff Moon spent many years as a teacher and teacher educator specializing in reading. He has written more than 140 books for children and teachers and he reviews regularly for teachers' journals.

The four levels of *Eyewitness Readers* are aimed at different reading abilities, enabling you to choose the books that are exactly right for your child.

Level One   Beginning to read
Level Two   Beginning to read alone
Level Three Reading alone
Level Four Proficient readers

The "normal" age at which a child begins to read can be anywhere from three to eight years old, so these levels are intended only as a general guideline.

No matter which level you select, you can be sure that you're helping your child learn to read, then read to learn!

A Dorling Kindersley Book

Project Editor Carey Combe
Art Editor Karen Lieberman
Senior Editor Linda Esposito
Senior Art Editor Andrew Burgess
Production Josie Alabaster
Picture Researcher Jamie Robinson
Illustrators Malcolm McGregor
and Peter Dennis

Reading Consultant
Cliff Moon M.Ed.

Published in Great Britain by
Dorling Kindersley Limited
9 Henrietta Street
London WC2E 8PS

4 6 8 10 9 7 5 3

Visit us on the World Wide Web at http://www.dk.com

A CIP catalogue record for this book is
available from the British Library.
ISBN 0-7513-5859-2

Colour reproduction by Colourscan, Singapore
Printed and bound in Belgium by Proost

The publisher would like to thank the following for their kind permission
to reproduce their photographs:
a=above; c=centre; b=below/bottom; l=left; r=right; t=top

Ardea London: Kev Deacon 11 b, 13; P. Morris 7;
D. Parer & E. Parer-Cook 19 tl; Ron & Valerie Taylor 11 c, 12, 15 cl,
18, 19 tr, 25 t, 28 b, 29 cl, br, 30 t, cl, 37 br, 38 c, 40 tr;
Adrian Warren 19 b; **Bruce Coleman Ltd**: Michael Glover 37 tr;
Mary Evans Picture Library: 14 br; **The Ronald Grant Archive**: *Jaws:
The Revenge*, 1987 © MCA/Universal Pictures 14 bl; **T. Britt Griswold**:
38 bl; **Innerspace Visions**: Kurt Amsler 41 b; Bob Cranston 25 b;
Nigel Marsh 40 bl; Doug Perrine 46 t; **Oxford Scientific films**: Richard
Herrmann 37 cl; **Pictor International**: 41 tr; **Planet Earth Pictures**:
F. J. Jackson 27; Doug Perrine 15 b, 28 t, 42 cl; Marty Snyderman 10;
James D. Watt 38–39, 47; Norbert Wu 15 cr; **Science Photo Library**:
BSIP LECA 44; Eye of Science 35; **Smithsonian Institution**, NMNH:
Chip Clark 33 outer; **Waterhouse stock Photography**: Stephen Frink 45;
Wild Images: Howard Hall 31.
Jacket: **Telegraph Colour Library**: front cover main.

Contents

Shark attack!   4

Shark attacks – the facts   14

Sharks and safety   24

Sharks up close   32

Sharks under attack   40

Glossary   48

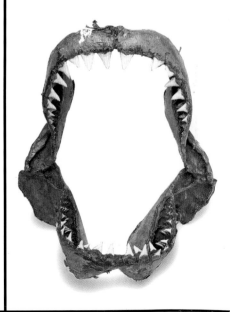

EYEWITNESS ◉ READERS

Level
3
READING ALONE

SHARK ATTACK!

Written by Cathy East Dubowski

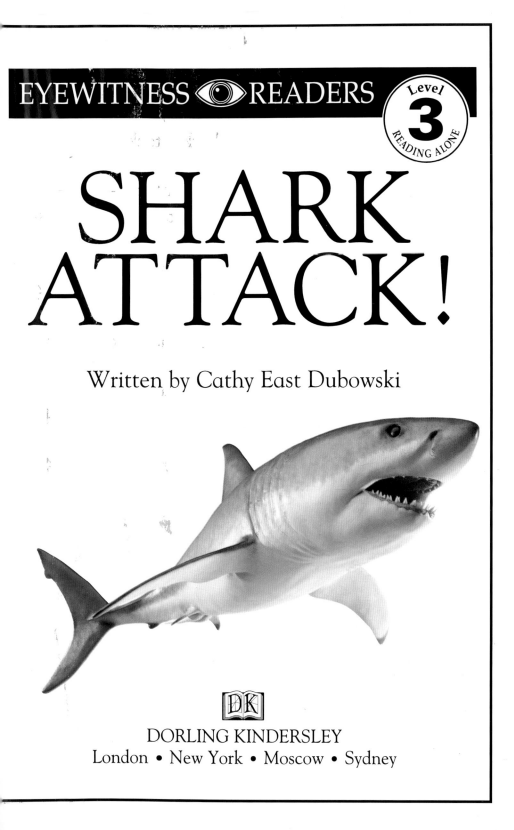

DK

DORLING KINDERSLEY
London • New York • Moscow • Sydney

Shark attack!

Rodney Fox had almost run out of time. He needed to find a big fish – and he needed to find it soon. The young Australian was competing in an annual spear fishing championship. To win he had to find and spear a big local fish. Rodney had won the contest last year and he wanted to win again. But today something was about to happen that would change his life forever.

Like all the other competitors, Rodney wore a long line attached to his diving-belt to hold the fish he had caught.

Shark capital!

Australia has the highest number of shark attacks in the world. But even so, since 1901 there have been fewer than 300 attacks.

AUSTRALIA

He and the other divers had been diving for several hours. They had caught a lot of fish and the water smelt of blood.

About one kilometre (half a mile) offshore, Rodney saw a huge morwong – just the fish he needed to win! Carefully, he aimed his spear gun at the fish.

CRASH! Something slammed hard into Rodney's side. He felt as if he had been hit by an express train!

It was a great white shark! The force of the impact knocked the mask off Rodney's face and the spear gun from his hand. His left shoulder disappeared down the creature's throat. Then the shark bit down on Rodney's chest and back.

Rodney struggled to get free. He hit the shark with his fist. But the shark held tight and shook him from side to side.

Then Rodney remembered the weakest spot on a shark's body – its eyes. With all his strength he rammed his right fist straight into the shark's eye. Incredibly, the shark let go.

Sharks' eyes

To protect its eyes from attack, a shark can roll them back into its head. Some sharks have a special membrane that covers the eyeball like a window blind.

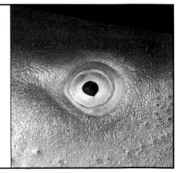

Bleeding and running out of air, Rodney struggled towards the surface. Could he make it to safety before the great white shark ate him alive?

Rodney reached the surface and gasped for air. He'd made it! But then he looked down. The shark was racing straight for him. Its huge jaws, lined with razor-sharp teeth, were wide open!

SNAP! The shark's jaws slammed shut again. But this time the shark swallowed the fish attached to Rodney's diving-belt. Suddenly, Rodney felt himself being pulled through the water – he was still attached to the line!

The shark began to drag him down into deep water. He struggled to undo his diving-belt but the buckle had slipped round his back. He couldn't reach it.

Time was running out. If the shark didn't eat him, Rodney would drown.

Suddenly the line snapped. Rodney was free! He struggled to the surface and shouted for help. Luckily, friends in a nearby boat had seen Rodney in distress and quickly pulled him out of the water.

Rodney was seriously hurt. His rib cage, lungs and the upper part of his stomach lay open from the huge gash where the shark had sunk its teeth in. The bite had crushed his ribs and punctured one of his lungs.

Rodney Fox is one of the few people to have survived the bite of a great white shark.

Rodney was rushed to the nearest hospital. Four hours of surgery and 462 stitches saved his life. But he would wear the ugly scar of the shark's bite forever.

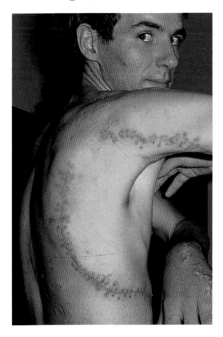

The attack on Rodney was big news. The public, frightened of more attacks, demanded action to clear the local beaches of sharks. But Rodney thought differently.

Deadly teeth

A shark's mouth has up to six rows of triangular teeth. When one tooth falls out, another takes its place. A great white shark has up to 100 teeth.

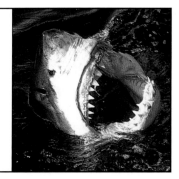

Rodney didn't want to go out and kill sharks – he wanted to go out and learn more about the mysterious creature that had nearly killed him. And he began a lifelong search to discover more about these silent hunters of the deep.

Only a few months after the attack, Rodney was diving again. So that he could get close to sharks, Rodney designed and built the first shark cage.

Rodney Fox now dives with sharks and is trying to save them from extinction.

A shark cage is about the size of a small lift. It is made of very strong metal bars, which are placed close enough together to keep a shark from biting the divers inside but still allow the divers a good view of the shark. Floats at the top keep the cage from sinking.

Today many people use shark cages. They allow divers and scientists to study and photograph sharks close up – but not quite as close as Rodney once came! ❖

Shark attacks – the facts

If you're terrified of sharks, you're not alone. Shark attacks make frightening headlines and movies like *Jaws* spread the fear that sharks are bloodthirsty killers. In fact, just the thought of sharks is enough to scare many people.

But the truth is that shark attacks are actually very rare. A person is far more likely to be hit by a car or struck by lightning than be attacked by a shark.

Popular fiction has helped spread false fears about sharks.

There are over 350 different species – or types – of sharks. Only about 30 of these species have ever been known to attack humans. But there are three that are really dangerous: the great white shark, the bull shark and the tiger shark.

A tiger shark is large and powerful enough to attack most sea creatures.

Bull sharks are one of the few sharks that can live in both fresh and sea water.

The great white shark is the most feared and fearsome of all sharks. It has even been known to attack boats.

Whether or not you are in danger of a shark attack depends on where you live in the world. Sharks are found almost everywhere but they seem to prefer warm water. Most shark attacks happen in Australia, Brazil, California, Florida, Hawaii and South Africa. They often occur near crowded beaches where people go to swim, sail and surf.

This symbol shows the location of fatal shark attacks since records began.

But even in a very bad year, sharks attack no more than 80 to 100 people in the whole world. Modern transport methods and improved medical care mean that only 10 to 15 of these people die.

Even then, sharks don't usually set out to attack people. Often they ignore people in the water. So what makes a shark attack a human?

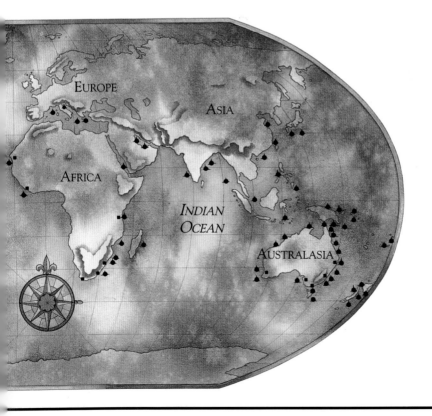

Some people believe that sharks attack when they feel threatened. A diver may unknowingly swim into a shark's territory. In this case, a shark may only bite a human once. It will then release – rather than eat – the invader. Perhaps this is what happened to diver Henry Bource. A single bite from a large shark resulted in him losing a leg. Divers are sometimes attacked while carrying fish they have caught. The blood and frantic movements of the dying fish attract sharks, who can smell blood from a great distance.

Henry Bource

A shark's view of a seal and a surfer from below

Sometimes a shark attack could be a case of mistaken identity. From a shark's point of view, a surfer on a surfboard looks like its favourite food – a seal. Once the shark tastes the board, it will spit it out and go away. Many surfers are still alive to tell the tale, with a munched surfboard to prove it!

A 4-metre (13-foot) tiger shark bit this surfer's board in Hawaii, USA.

An attack may happen because a shark is hungry. Experts think that Raymond Short was attacked by a hungry shark while swimming in the water off a crowded Australian beach.

Raymond was swimming near the shore when he was bitten by a shark. Six lifeguards immediately dashed into the sea to save him. But as they started to carry Raymond towards the shore the lifeguards realized that the shark was still attached to Raymond's leg!

Raymond had
to be pulled right
onto the beach
before the shark
let go of his leg.

The shark had a long wound along
its stomach. It had been badly injured.
Scientists think that the shark had been
unable to catch its normal food and was
so hungry it took unusual risks.

Another strange attack took place in a very unexpected place – a creek!

Twelve-year-old Lester Stilwell was swimming with his friends in Matawan Creek in New Jersey, USA. Suddenly he screamed and disappeared beneath the water. A man named Stanley Fisher rushed into the creek to drag Lester's lifeless body from the water. Suddenly Stanley felt something bump his right leg. When he reached down he realized part of his leg had been ripped away.

They had been attacked by a shark! Tragically both died from their wounds.

But was this attack really so strange? Not if you know anything about sharks. Even though the shark was never found, it was most likely a bull shark, a species that lives in both salt and fresh water. ❖

Sharks and safety

People have tried many ways to protect themselves from shark attacks as they explore the shark's watery world.

One of the most popular methods of protecting swimmers is simply to build a fence, or shark net, in the water. These shark nets are used off many popular Australian and South African beaches. But the nets cost a lot of money to build and need frequent repairs.

Shark nets are set up off popular beaches.

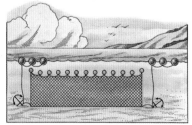

Nets stop sharks from swimming into an area.

Electrical beach barriers are also being tested, as sharks won't swim through strong electric currents.

A big problem with shark nets is that they trap and kill all types of sharks, as well as other creatures like dolphins.

If you visit a shark zone:

- Don't swim if you have a bleeding cut. Sharks can smell blood more than 1.6 kilometres (1 mile) away.
- Don't swim at dusk as this is the time when sharks are likely to be feeding.
- Don't urinate in the sea. Sharks are attracted to the smell.
- Never swim alone.
- Get out of the water if a shark is sighted.

MUNICIPALITY OF ROCKDALE

DANGER

SHARKS IN BOTANY BAY

People who are victims of shipwrecks or plane crashes at sea are often at risk of being attacked by a shark because they are so far from land.

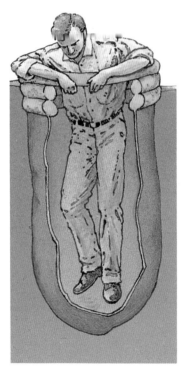

One invention to protect people floating in the sea is the shark screen bag. It is like a large plastic bag, which is closed at the bottom and has floats at the top. When not in use, it is small enough to be folded up and tucked into a pocket. But when inflated, the bag hides the person's shape, movement, smells and sounds from passing sharks, hopefully keeping the person safe until help arrives.

Many people have tried to invent a chemical shark repellent. During World War II many soldiers were killed by sharks when their ships sank. The army tried to make a repellent made of chemicals and dye. It was meant to repel sharks, as well as hide the person from view. But it didn't work, as it dissolved too quickly.

One of the latest ideas is to try to copy the poison made by a fish called the moses sole. If caught by a shark, the fish squirts out poison. Sharks hate the taste so much, they spit the fish out!

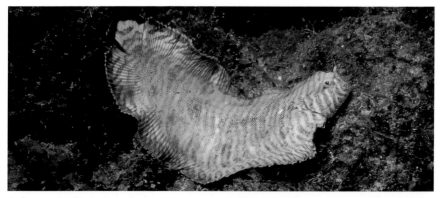

Moses soles are slow swimmers. Their poison protects them.

Divers who dive for sport or to study and film underwater life often come face to face with dangerous sharks. Some carry spear guns, or bangsticks that fire a small explosive charge that can kill a shark. But for those who want to study sharks, killing them is not the answer.

A bangstick can kill a large shark immediately.

Valerie and Ron Taylor developed a new idea. These Australian film makers are well known for their underwater photography. But it is dangerous work. Valerie has the shark bites to prove it!

On one diving trip, the Taylors  noticed a crew member wearing some stainless-steel mesh gloves to protect his hands while cleaning fish. This gave them an idea. Why not make a whole diving-suit out of chain-mail to protect divers from sharks – like the chain-mail suits worn by knights?

They made a suit out of 400,000 tiny stainless-steel rings. But to test the suit, someone had to wear it in the water. Someone had to make the sharks bite!

Saving their skins
Small rings on a chain-mail suit stop a shark's teeth from biting through skin. But the diver will still be bruised.

Valerie in her chain-mail suit

The Taylors carried out a test dive off the coast of California. Raw chunks of fish were dumped into the water to attract sharks. Valerie Taylor zipped up the chain-mail suit over her normal diving-suit and then dived into the water among the raw chunks of fish.

Soon several sharks darted in. Valerie waved a bleeding fish close to her body, baiting the sharks to bite. Suddenly a shark chomped down on Valerie's arm! She was startled, but not hurt.

The shark bit her again and again all over her body. It was frightening but the shark's teeth couldn't get through the mesh. The suit had worked!

But there had been some anxious moments. One shark had pulled off one of Valerie's gloves and bitten her thumb. Luckily, Valerie had managed to escape.

The suit needed small improvements. But thanks to Valerie's bravery, the first practical shark suit had been invented! ❖

Diver protected from a shark attack by his chain-mail suit

The shark is perfectly evolved for surviving and hunting underwater. Its amazingly flexible body is due to a skeleton made of cartilage – the same material that forms our noses and ears!

A shark has the same five senses as a human – sight, hearing, smell, taste and touch. But the shark's ability to catch prey in murky waters is due to two extra, and very unusual, senses.

The dorsal fin helps balance and steering.

Pectoral fins act as brakes.

The caudal fin keeps the shark from rolling over.

Gills take oxygen from the water.

Running down each side of a shark's body is a "lateral line". This is a line of pressure-sensitive points under the skin, which help the shark sense small vibrations in the water.

On the head of a shark are tiny pores called the ampullae of Lorenzini. They allow a shark to sense the faint electrical charges given off by all living things.

Sharks can hear up to 836 metres (1,000 feet) away.

Sharks can see up to 42 metres (50 feet) away.

Ampullae of Lorenzini (am-POOL-i of lor-un-ZEE-nee)

Shark skin

Shark skin is covered with tiny tooth-like scales. Before sandpaper, shark skin was used to smooth down wood!

Sharks are solitary animals – they live, swim and hunt alone. Scientists know very little about their life cycle. What is known, however, is that sharks are very slow to reproduce. Some sharks take 11 years before they are ready to mate. And when sharks do give birth, they often have few babies. So sharks take extra care to protect their eggs.

Many lay their eggs in tough protective egg cases. Others give birth to live babies called pups. To help them survive, these pups are already quite big when they are born.

Egg cases

Shark pups

Sharks eat most kinds of food – but all sharks eat meat. Many eat small fish and animals like lobsters and jellyfish,

Basking shark

although tin cans and plastic bags have also been found in a shark's stomach! Some larger sharks hunt bigger animals,

Jellyfish

such as seals, penguins and even other sharks. A few, like the basking shark, simply swim along with their mouths wide open. They catch plankton, the tiny plant and animal life found in the ocean, as well as small animals such as shrimps.

Seals

Do you think you know what a shark looks like? Maybe you should think again! When most people think of sharks, they imagine the classic shape of the great white shark. But sharks come in all sizes and some extremely unusual shapes. All the sharks below are shown in proportion.

Hammerhead shark

Lantern shark

Angel shark

The biggest shark is the whale shark. It can grow up to 12.2 metres (40 feet) long and weigh as much as 13.2 tonnes (13 tons) making it the largest fish in the world. The world's smallest shark is the lantern shark. It grows no larger than 20 centimetres (8 inches)! It is known as the lantern shark because its eyes glow in the dark! ❖

Wobbegong shark

Horn shark

Whale shark

Sharks under attack

For centuries people have feared sharks. But, today, sharks have much more to fear from people. Overfishing is threatening many species with extinction.

Shark's tooth necklace

Sharks have been hunted for many years. Their flesh and teeth were used for weapons, food and even jewellery but the numbers caught posed no threat to the shark population.

Today, modern fishing methods mean that sharks are killed in huge numbers – up to 100 million sharks every year.

As a result, the population of some sharks may have dropped by as much as 80 per cent in the last ten years.

Often the sharks are killed by accident because they get trapped in fishing nets. The fishermen keep the fish they want and throw the unwanted sharks back into the ocean – dead.

Much shark killing is just for sport. People who hunt and kill a shark may seem brave but they are never in any danger. The jaws make flashy trophies that sell to tourists for lots of money.

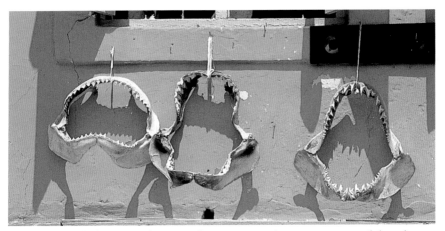

This shark hunter hangs his victims' jaws around his boat.

Shark meal

Sharks are also under attack because, in many parts of the world, people eat shark meat. In Asia, shark-fin soup is an expensive treat Fishermen can earn so much money from shark fins that, when they catch a shark, they hack off its fins and throw the dying animal back into the water.

Fins from any type of shark are used to make shark-fin soup.

In some countries shark cartilage is made into health pills. Some people believe that the pills will cure almost anything, from heart disease to cancer. Nearly all of these claims are false.

Shark skin is also tanned and made into very expensive leather belts and wallets.

Modern shark leather box

One of the most valuable shark products is its liver. The oil taken from a shark's liver is used in many products, including industrial oils and medicines. The oil was also used to make vitamin A pills until a different source was found in the 1950s.

Vitamin A tablets

Cruel creams

The gall bladder and liver of sharks are still used to make beauty creams, even though natural plant oils could be used instead.

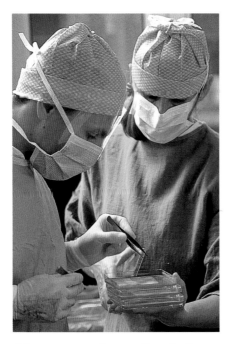

Doctors with artificial skin grown from shark cartilage

If we don't control the mass killing of sharks, they may become extinct. But why would this matter?

Scientists have discovered many amazing things about sharks and we have a great deal to learn from this ancient creature. Sharks may even save our lives one day.

For instance, researchers have found that squaline, a chemical made in the liver and stomach of the dogfish shark, slows down the growth of tumours in humans. And shark cartilage is now used to make artificial skin for burn patients.

Sharks also have highly developed immune systems – which means they don't often fall ill. Their cuts and wounds heal very quickly. And they rarely get cancer like other animals, even when scientists inject cancer cells into sharks' bodies in laboratory tests.

Why? Scientists don't know yet. But studying sharks may help doctors cure people who are sick.

This great white shark has been cut by struggling prey, but the wounds will soon heal.

Aquariums are safe places to go and see a shark!

The more we learn about sharks, the more we will learn to admire and respect them. Of course most people don't want to come face to face with a great white shark in the ocean – like Rodney Fox!

But we can visit sharks in aquariums and watch fascinating films made by underwater film makers. We can even take trips to see sharks in the sea.

Sharks are fascinating, intelligent and graceful creatures. Only a few kinds of sharks are dangerous. Attacks on people are really very rare. The shark's reputation as a bloodthirsty killer is not accurate or fair.

Sharks have had a home on our planet far longer than we have. It would be a real shame if people made them disappear from our seas forever. ❖

Glossary

Ampullae of Lorenzini
(am-POOL-i of lor-un-ZEE-nee)
Tiny pores on a shark's head that can detect faint electrical signals in the water.

Aquarium
A large tank where sea animals are kept so people can view them safely.

Bangstick
An underwater gun that fires a small explosive charge that is strong enough to kill a large shark.

Carcharodon megalodon
(car-CARE-oh-don MEG-a-loh-don)
The largest shark that ever lived in the sea. It died out over 10 million years ago.

Cartilage
A tough, flexible material from which a shark's skeleton is made. Human noses and ears are also made of cartilage.

Chain-mail suit
A diving-suit made up of thousands of tiny interlocking stainless-steel rings. It protects divers from shark bites.

Denticles
The tiny tooth-like scales that cover a shark's skin.

Extinction
When a particular animal or plant dies out completely.

Fossils
The remains of plants and animals that lived millions of years ago. Fossils are often in rocks.

Lateral line
A line of points along each side of a shark's body that help sharks sense vibrations in the water.

Moses sole
A slow fish that releases a poisonous liquid when caught.

Plankton
Tiny animals and plants that live in the sea.

Shark cage
A small metal cage that protects divers.

Shark chaser
A mix of chemicals and dye shaped into a cake. It was meant to protect people from sharks.

Shark net
A net that is hung under the water to stop sharks from attacking swimmers off a beach.

Shark screen bag
An inflatable bag that hides shipwreck victims from sharks by hiding any smells or movements.

Spear fishing
Fishing underwater with a spear gun.

Spear gun
An underwater gun that fires spears. It is used by underwater divers to catch fish.

Squaline
A valuable chemical found in a shark's liver. Humans use it for a number of medical reasons.